j389   Nation, Kay.
Nat   Meters, liters, and grams; understanding
        the metric system. [By] Kay and Bob
        Nation.   Illus. by Lynn Sweat.   New York,
        Hawthorn Books, 1975.
           64 p.   illus.

        1. Metric system.   I. Title.

                                        A-5724 LC

METERS,
LITERS, AND
GRAMS

METERS, LITERS, AND GRAMS

Understanding the Metric System

Kay and Bob Nation

Illustrated by Lynn Sweat

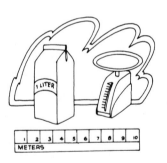

HAWTHORN BOOKS, INC.
Publishers/New York

For Nancy Coover

Contents

1
Meet Mark, Jackie, and the Metric System

MEET MARK, WHO is twelve years old. He is 150 centimeters tall and weighs 40 kilograms. His younger sister, Jackie, is 145 centimeters tall and weighs 36 kilograms.

Sound strange? Soon you may be giving similar information about yourself using metric terms. With Mark and Jackie, you will discover how to measure almost everything in a new and easier way —the metric way.

Why bother to change, you ask? Why not do it the way we do now? We will discuss the reasons for changing and then you can make up your own mind which way is best.

First, it's easier to figure things out using metric units because you are using a decimal system. Many times you can get an answer simply by adding a zero or moving a decimal point. Mark and Jackie will show you how.

COUNTRIES
NOT USING
METRIC SYSTEM

The second reason for changing is that the United States is one of the few countries in the world not already using the metric system, as you can see by looking at this map.

When we trade with other countries, our measurements confuse them. For instance, when we order 100 pounds of butter they may send us 100 kilograms instead, as their scales are all based on the metric gram. To avoid this mistake, they have to figure out how many kilograms equal 100 pounds. This is costly and time-consuming for them and for us, as we have to do the same when shipping items to other countries.

Did you know that many people in the United States are already using the metric system today? Doctors, druggists, and scientists in many fields are using it every day.

This brings us to the third reason for changing to the metric way. Most people agree it is necessary to have one basic system of measuring, and it is logical to make it the system already used by most of the world and some of our citizens.

The metric system began with the French, back in 1790. After the French Revolution, the new government wanted a different way of doing almost everything. So the Paris Academy of Sciences was asked to construct a new system of weights and measures based on the most advanced scientific principles of the time. A group of scientists, including Pierre Simon Laplace and Antoine Laurent Lavoisier, decided to make the new standard of length an unchanging portion of the Earth's surface. The portion used was the distance from the North Pole to the equator, which is a quarter of the distance around the Earth and is called a quadrant. The quadrant then was divided into 10 million equal parts. Each of these parts was called a meter, derived from the French word for measure. All other units of length measurement were based on the meter, so anyone knowing the length of a meter could easily figure out other measurements.

The French scientists decided to make this new system so easy to use that everyone would adopt it. So they made it a decimal system. The Latin word *decem* means ten, and multiplying and dividing by 10 is much faster than figuring in units of 12 or 36 as we have to do with inches, feet, and yards. In the metric system, each unit is 10 times larger than the next smallest unit, and 10 times smaller than the next largest unit. The French developed a similar system for measuring weight and volume. They went so far as to live on a 10-day week for a while during the Revolution, but they gave that up and went back to the 7-day week.

By 1795, laws had been passed requiring everyone in France to use the new metric way of measuring. An international conference was held in Paris to tell other nations what had been done and to show them the new standards.

Not all the French people wanted to change. They liked the old way better because they were more familiar with it. Besides, butchers had their own scales to weigh meat and bakers had their own to weigh bread. None of the scales were alike so people never knew exactly how much they were getting, but most shopkeepers didn't want to buy new scales just to be accurate.

So the people in France went on using the old ways until finally, in 1812, Napoleon issued a decree that said people could use some of the old

system and some of the new metric system. This gave the people time to become familiar with the new way, and after 25 years the metric system became the more popular one. In 1837, a law was passed making the metric system the only system to be used in France after January 1, 1840.

Other countries saw how well this system was working for France, and by 1850 the Netherlands, Greece, Spain, and parts of Italy had adopted it. By 1880, seventeen other nations, including most of South America, had changed to the metric way. Today only a few countries in the world do *not* use it.

What was the United States doing through all this time? We were gradually drifting toward metric measurement. Your doctor writes out a prescription for you using metric terms, and your druggist fills it that way. If you become a scientist someday, you will find that the language and tools of science are almost entirely metric. How about the mechanic who fixes cars? He has to have metric tools to work on cars made in other countries. Since our country is thinking more and more in metric terms, Mark and Jackie need to know not only where this metric system came from but how it works.

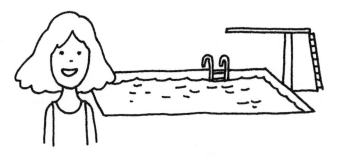

Jackie is a good swimmer. She has won every meet she has competed in and broken two records along the way. Her brother, not to be outdone, has worked long and hard in his specialty, track. He already has qualified for the track team and is dreaming about winning a medal in the district meet.

Mark has been training for the 100-meter race at school. The distance was measured off for him by his track coach, so he never thought about how it was measured. Now that the district track meet is getting closer, he would like to practice at home, too. In the next chapter, you and Mark will learn how to measure distance.

Everything is related in the metric system, so there are only a few new things to learn.

UNITS OF MEASURE	PREFIXES
meter	*milli* means 1/1,000
liter	*centi* means 1/100
gram	*deci* means 1/10
	kilo means 1,000

2
Measuring Distances

MARK IS BUSY getting ready for the track meet. The coach feels he has a good chance of winning if he can cut his time by just a little, so each day Mark has been practicing after school. He marked off his track at home with a yardstick, but his running time was so fast that he knew he must have made a mistake. When Mark asked his coach about it, the coach reminded him that the school track was measured in meters and that a meter is longer than a yard. Let's compare a meter with a yard to see how they differ.

1	2	3	4	5	6	7	8	9	10

I METER

	1		2		3

I YARD

The yard is divided into feet and inches. The meter is divided into units called centimeters and there are 100 of them in a meter, just as there are 100 cents in a dollar. The abbreviation for centimeter is cm.

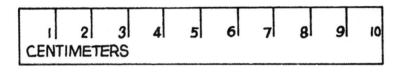

If you make a copy of the ruler on this page, you can measure yourself and the objects around you, as well as the ones shown here in the book. How many centimeters long is the pen? The comb?

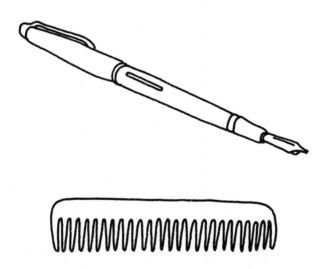

Now you can measure your height in centimeters and compare it to Mark's and Jackie's. Stand against the wall and make a mark to show your height. Then use the 10-centimeter ruler to measure the distance from the floor to the mark on the wall. Are you as tall as Mark, or is Jackie more your size?

Mark is 150 centimeters tall, but we also could say he is 15 decimeters tall. Jackie is 14.5 decimeters tall. A decimeter is made up of 10 centimeters, as our foot is made up of 12 inches. But it is easier to change centimeters to decimeters than inches to feet. Can you see why? It is easier to divide by 10, isn't it? All you have to do is move the decimal point one place to the left. A decimeter is this long:

The abbreviation for decimeter is dm. There are 10 decimeters in 1 meter, just as there are 10 dimes in 1 dollar. And you can remember there are 10 centimeters in 1 decimeter—the same as 10 cents in 1 dime. Now you can tell your height in decimeters, too—by dividing the number of centimeters by 10.

Since there are 100 cm in 1 meter, you now know by what to divide 150 cm in order to tell Mark's height in meters. Right, you just divide by 100, which you can do by moving the decimal point two places to the left. That makes Mark 1.5 meters tall and Jackie 1.45 meters tall. Once you catch on, the metric system is much easier than changing feet to yards or inches to feet, as there aren't so many different numbers to multiply and divide.

Sometimes there are tiny objects, smaller than a centimeter, that you might want to measure. On this page is a ruler that will do just that. It is marked off in millimeters. It takes 10 millimeters to make 1 centimeter and 1,000 millimeters to make 1 meter. A millimeter is so small that it takes about 25 of them to make 1 inch. You can write 1 millimeter as 1 mm.

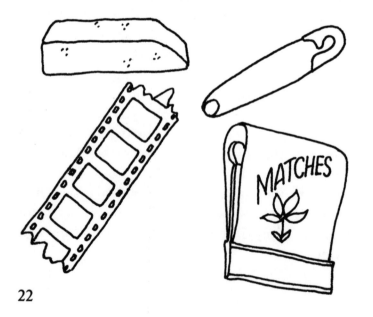

Using a copy of the ruler on this page, you can measure the objects shown here in the book and other small items around your house.

What did you get for the length of the safety pin? What about the book of matches? The eraser is 40 mm long. The movie projector used in most schools is a 16 mm projector, which means that the film is 16 mm wide.

Before we go back to see how Mark is doing with his track, let's review the units of length smaller than a meter.

$$1 \text{ meter (m)} = 1,000 \text{ millimeters (mm)}$$
$$1 \text{ meter (m)} = 100 \text{ centimeters (cm)}$$
$$1 \text{ meter (m)} = 10 \text{ decimeters (dm)}$$

Now let's compare Mark's new 100-meter track laid out beside the 100-yard one he did first. No wonder his times were better on the 100-yard track. Look how much shorter it is.

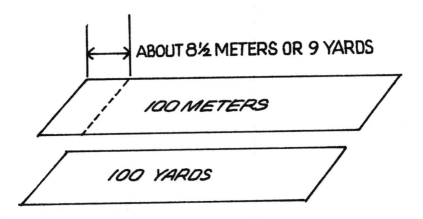

Let's use metric measurement to figure out how far Mark will have to travel to get to the district meet in Colorado Springs. He and Jackie live in Denver, Colorado, which is 75 miles from Colorado Springs. But the metric system uses kilometers instead of miles to measure longer distances.

First, we need to know how long a kilometer is. Since everything else in the metric system is based on the meter, we would expect the kilometer to be, too. And it is. A kilometer is 1,000 meters. Or you could write it as 1 km = 1,000 m. As you can see in the drawing below, a kilometer is much shorter than a mile.

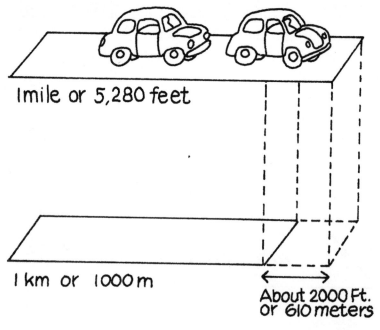

1mile or 5,280 feet

1 km or 1000 m

About 2000 Ft. or 610 meters

In many other countries, you would see road signs like these:

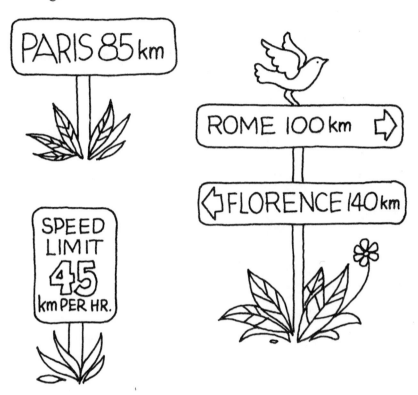

If you were traveling there, you would be given a chart that shows how many miles per hour equal how many kilometers per hour. Without this chart, it would be easy for you to break the speed limit when you go sight-seeing, unless your speedometer showed kilometers per hour instead of miles per hour.

Mark and his family leave Denver early in the morning on the day of the track meet. It's a beautiful drive, with the sun shining on the snow-capped peaks of the Rocky Mountains. A distance of 75 miles sounds shorter than 125 kilometers, but it is really the same and goes by quickly.

Finally it is time for Mark's race to begin. The grandstands are full of cheering people from all over the district. As the runners line up, Mark has the inside lane. He starts out well and is out in front until the runner from a nearby town pulls almost even with him. They are still together as they approach the finish line, so close that Mark's family doesn't know until the announcement that Mark came in first. He won the first-place medal and broke the meet record for the 100-meter race with a time of 11.2 seconds.

3

Exploring Perimeters and Areas

ONCE THE EXCITEMENT of the track meet is over, Mark is restless. He wonders how his speed can help him in another sport. He wants an exciting and challenging sport and decides that baseball might be a possibility.

Let's figure out how far Mark will have to run if he hits a home run. Using the baseball diamond shown, see if you can find the distance around it.

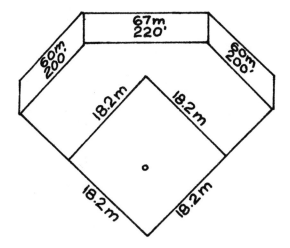

Perimeter means the total distance around a given area. So the perimeter of the diamond is 72.8 meters. Using a meter stick, you can find the perimeter of your kitchen table, this book, your room, or a window. Just add the lengths of the sides to find the total distance around. You can practice by finding the perimeters of the objects shown.

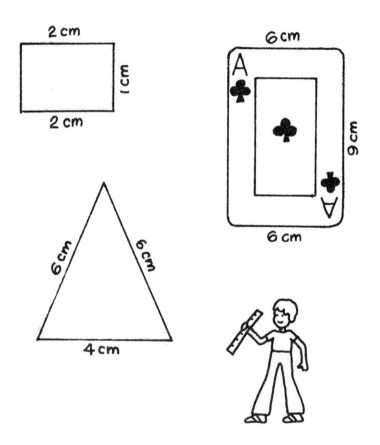

Did you find that the figure on the left has a perimeter of 6 cm? And that the perimeter of the playing card is 30 cm? What about the triangle?

Now that you know how to find the perimeter, let's discover how to measure area the metric way. We'll start by finding the area of a square. Let's use the baseball diamond as an example. You just multiply the length times the width. Since this is a square, you take one side times another side, or 18.2 times 18.2, to get 331.24 square meters.

A square meter is a square that is one meter long on each side. The baseball diamond contains 331.24 of these square meters. You can write square meter as sq m.

Let's try measuring something smaller and easier to work with. Here is a square centimeter (1 sq cm).

Now we will put a few of these areas together to form a rectangle. How many square centimeters are there in the rectangle?

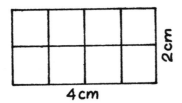

29

By counting, you can find 8 sq cm. There is an easier way to find out. If you multiply the length (4 cm) by the width (2 cm), you get the same total area as when you counted—8 sq cm. So when you want to find the area of a rectangle, you just multiply the length times the width. Why don't you try to find the area of the rectangles shown?

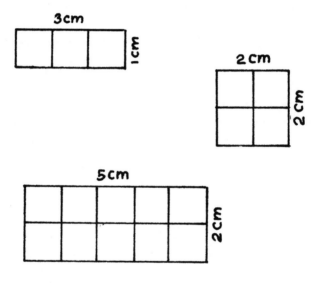

The first rectangle has an area of 3 sq cm, the second is a square with an area of 4 sq cm, and the third has an area of 10 sq cm.

Someday you might want to carpet your room. If the carpet is sold in square meters, you can figure out how much carpeting you need and how much it would cost. Jackie is working on this now. Her room is 5 meters long by 4 meters wide. If the carpeting costs $8 a square meter, how much would it cost to carpet her room?

5m

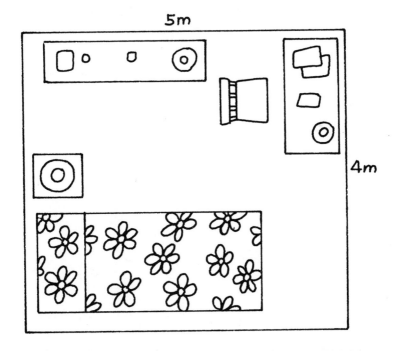

4m

The area of Jackie's room is 20 sq m, so it will cost her 20 times $8, or $160. That was easy to figure out—much easier than measuring in feet and then converting them into yards.

Someday everyone will figure out such things in this simpler metric way, and by then you will know how to do it. You already know how to measure

length and how to find the perimeter and area. It will just take some practice to be good at it, just as it takes practice to be good at almost anything.

Speaking of practice, Mark has been practicing his batting to be ready to try out for the baseball team. But he has been having some problems. He can run as fast as lightning and steal bases better than anyone on the team. The problem is that he can't hit the ball. Even after three weeks of practice, he misses many more balls than he hits.

When it's Mark's turn at bat in the tryouts, the first pitch is low and outside for a ball. Mark swings hard and misses the second pitch. Strike one. He misses the next one, too. Two strikes already. The next pitch is wild for a ball. Two balls and two strikes. One more ball, low and inside. The count is three and two. The last pitch looks good and Mark swings with all he has. Strike three, and Mark is out!

"Well, you can't be good at everything," Mark tells himself. He'll just have to find another interest.

His new minicycle is fun to ride, and he decides to ask some of his friends to bring their bikes so they can have races in the field across the street from his house.

While Mark is figuring distances for the cycle races, his dad and Jackie are planning to build a corral. Jackie has always wanted a pony. Her tenth birthday is coming up, and her parents have decided she's old enough now to take care of a pony.

Before they can get the pony, Jackie and her dad have to figure out how much fence they will have to buy for the corral. This gives Jackie a chance to make practical use of what she has learned about measuring perimeter and area in metric figures. Their home is located on 2.5 acres or 1 hectare (ha) of land. A hectare is any land area that contains 10,000 square meters. It can look like either of the figures below. Theirs happens to be a long, narrow piece of land rather than a square.

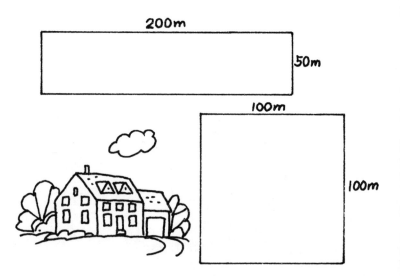

They stake off an area 50 m by 75 m and discover that there will be plenty of room for the pony to run around. By multiplying 50x75, they find that the corral will have an area of 3,750 sq m.

Now to find out how much fence they will need, they must find the perimeter of the corral. So they add 50 +75 +50 +75 and get a total of 250 meters.

As soon as the fencing is delivered, Jackie helps her father build a fence, knowing it won't be long until her very own pony will be running around the corral.

4

How to Measure Volume and Capacity

MARK HAS CHALLENGED Jackie to an unusual race. He wants to show her that his minicycle can go faster than her pony, Misty, even if the pony has a head start. Jackie likes the idea, but she needs time to get her pony ready.

Jackie was so thrilled to find a beautiful Shetland pony that she brought her home before everything was quite ready. The corral and a storage shed were already built, but now she needs a tank to hold water. She also needs to fill the storage shed with hay for Misty. To figure out how big a tank and how much hay she'll need, Jackie has to learn more about the new metric way of measuring.

Jackie's shed is 4 meters long by 2 meters wide by 3 meters high. To find out how much the shed will hold, you first have to know its volume, which is measured in cubic units. To find the volume of any container, you multiply length times width times height ($V = l \times w \times h$). So to find out how much the shed will hold, you take $4 \times 2 \times 3$ and get 24 cubic meters (cu m) or 24 m^3. This means that the shed will hold 24 cubes that are each 1 m long, 1 m wide, and 1 m high.

A cubic centimeter (cc or c³) is a small box because a centimeter is 1/100 of a meter. If you measure the cubic centimeter shown below, you can see that it is exactly 1 cm tall, 1 cm wide, and 1 cm long.

Why not try to find the volume of each of the boxes shown?

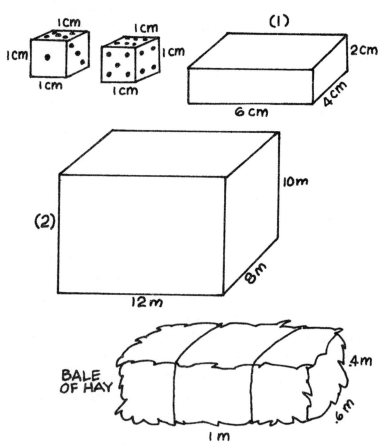

Did you get 1 cc for each of the dice? The first box is 48 cc and the second is 960 m³.

The bale of hay has a volume of .24m³. The volume of the shed is 24 m³. So to find out how many bales of hay the shed will hold, you divide 24m³ by .24 (the volume of 1 bale of hay). Your answer should be 100. So Jackie has room in her shed for 100 bales of hay.

There is one cubic unit that is especially important. This is a cubic decimeter (dm³). The reason it is so important is one of the things that makes the metric system fun and easy. A container that has a volume of dm³ will hold exactly 1 liter of liquid. A liter is slightly more than our quart. So under the metric system, instead of buying a quart of milk, you would buy a liter of milk.

1 quart   1 liter

All parts of the metric system work together. That way, many things can be figured out without changing units of measurement.

If you want to measure smaller amounts of liquid, as Jackie may want to in cooking, you use milliliters. One liter=1,000 milliliters (ml), or 1 ml=.001 liter. A teaspoon holds about 5 ml.

What if you want to measure amounts of liquid that are larger than liters? Then you use decaliters. One decaliter (dkl) = 10 liters. Instead of using gallons, you would use decaliters, only these are much bigger than our gallon. One dkl holds more than 2.5 gallons.

Now Jackie knows how to figure out what size water tank she needs for Misty. She knows a pony drinks about 40 liters of water a day. To be sure that Misty always has enough to drink, she decides her tank should hold about 400 liters.

A tank 5 dm high by 8 dm wide by 10 dm long would have a volume of 400 dm³. Since 1 dm³ = 1 liter, the tank should hold 400 liters.

8dm

5dm

10dm

Once Jackie has Misty all settled and provided for, she can get down to some serious practicing for the big race. If Mark gives her the 10-meter head start that he promised, she feels confident that she can beat that minicycle.

Mark, on the other hand, feels just as confident. He is always teasing Jackie about Misty being an old plug. He figures he'll pass Misty and finish the race while she is only at the halfway point.

Of course he doesn't tell Jackie that he has been working just as hard to get his minicycle in shape as she has to get Misty ready.

Mark filled up the minicycle with gas two days ago. The tank holds about 1 gallon or 3.8 liters. His instruction manual says that the minicycle gets 80 kilometers per liter. Now he needs to know how much gas he has left for the race today.

Mark drove a total of 32 kilometers yesterday riding through nearby fields. If he uses only 1 liter for every 80 kilometers, he should have more than 3 liters left. So he has plenty of gas.

On the day of the race, several of Mark's and Jackie's friends and neighbors gather at the edge of the field to watch the excitement.

Ready, set, go! The race is on. Jackie starts first, urging Misty on at a full gallop toward the line that marks the first 10 meters. As soon as Jackie and Misty reach that line, Mark takes off, coming up fast behind them.

At the halfway point, Jackie is still way ahead, but Mark is gaining. Misty hears the minicycle coming and she looks as though she has decided to beat that noisy machine. She really stretches out.

As they near the finish line, Misty is still out in front. Mark is going full speed, but it isn't fast enough. Jackie spurs Misty on, and with one last burst of speed they cross the finish line first. Jackie has won.

5

Lifting Weights, Measuring Weights

MARK HAS DECIDED to take up weight lifting. His goal is to be able to lift 20 kilograms by Christmas. But what's a kilogram?

In the metric system, weight is measured in grams. Since kilo means 1,000, a kilogram is 1,000 grams. That doesn't help much, does it? First we need to know how much a gram is.

Like everything else in the metric way of measuring, the gram is related to other units of measurement. You have already learned most of these. Remember: 1 cc of water equals 1 ml, and 1,000 ml equal 1 liter. This same 1 cc of water weighs 1 gram. You can write 1 gram as 1 g. So 1,000 cc of water (the same as 1,000 ml) weigh 1,000 g. This means that a liter of water weighs 1,000 g or 1 kilogram. A kilogram can be abbreviated as kg.

Now that you can see how all these measurements are related, let's look at some familiar objects to compare weights. A nickel weighs about 5 g, a can of soup weighs about 320 g, and a pound of butter weighs about 454 g.

If you look in your kitchen cupboard, you can find the weights of many other items listed in grams. Lift some of them and you can actually feel the weight of a certain number of grams. That gives you a better idea than just reading about it. It will take awhile to change your way of thinking, but before long it will seem natural to say, "I need a kilogram of butter."

When you buy butter by the kilogram, you will be getting more than you now get when you buy a pound of butter since 1 kg is about 2.2 pounds.

Mark has quite a job ahead of him. He will be lifting about 44 pounds when he lifts those 20-kg weights.

There are two other ways of measuring weight that you may need to know. You don't often weigh an airplane, but if you did, you would give its weight in metric tons. Another name for 1,000 kilograms is 1 metric ton (t). You also could write 1 t=1,000 kg. Once again, you can see how all types of measurements are related in the metric system.

One cubic meter of water weighs 1 metric ton. One cu m would be equal to 1,000 cu dm or 1,000 liters. Since 1 liter of water weighs 1 kilogram, 1,000 liters would weigh 1,000 kg. Amazing, isn't it?

The second term you may need someday is milligram (mg). This term can be used in giving the weight of something as tiny as a fly. It takes 1,000 mg to equal 1 gram.

While Mark practices lifting weights, Jackie experiments with metric weights in a different way. She decides to bake some chocolate chip cookies. It will give her a chance to practice all that she has been learning about the metric system in her science class at school.

Jackie's teacher, Ms. Wright, has been interested in the metric system for some time. She lived in France for two years and found out how much easier it was to measure recipe ingredients the metric way.

Ms. Wright has been telling Jackie and her classmates to think metric. For instance, a toothbrush is about 1 centimeter wide and a teaspoon contains nearly 5 milliliters.

Ms. Wright also has shown the class that weighing ingredients in recipes is much faster and simpler than sifting, packing, and leveling measuring cups full of the same ingredients.

Jackie has two recipes for chocolate chip cookies. One is her mother's and the other is a metric recipe Ms. Wright gave her.

Regular Chocolate Chip Cookies

½ cup plus 1 tablespoon sifted flour
¼ teaspoon soda
¼ teaspoon salt
¼ cup butter or margarine
3 tablespoons granulated sugar
3 tablespoons brown sugar
¼ teaspoon vanilla
¼ teaspoon water
1 egg
½ (6-ounce) package of chocolate pieces
¼ cup chopped nuts

Sift flour, soda, and salt together. Cream butter, granulated sugar, brown sugar, vanilla, and water together until fluffy. Beat in egg. Add flour mixture and mix well. Stir in chocolate pieces and chopped nuts. Drop by scant spoonfuls onto an ungreased cookie sheet. Bake at 350 degrees for 10 to 12 minutes or until brown. Makes about 2 dozen.

Metric Chocolate Chip Cookies

70	grams flour
2	grams soda
1	gram salt
45	grams butter or margarine
25	grams granulated sugar
40	grams brown sugar
2	milliliters vanilla
2	milliliters water
1	egg
75	grams chocolate pieces
30	grams chopped nuts

Sift flour, soda, and salt together. Cream butter, granulated sugar, brown sugar, vanilla, and water together until fluffy. Beat in egg. Add flour mixture and mix well. Stir in chocolate pieces and chopped nuts. Drop by scant spoonfuls onto ungreased cookie sheet. Bake at 177 degrees Celsius for 10 to 12 minutes or until brown. Makes about 2 dozen.

Both recipes have the same mixing directions. Only the quantities and baking temperatures seem to differ. Jackie decides it would be fun to try the metric recipe.

Jackie has the cookies all mixed and ready to bake. But what is this 177 degrees Celsius? She has always baked cookies at about 350 degrees.

Where should she set the oven temperature? Perhaps you can help her figure it out.

The Celsius (C) or centigrade scale for temperature is commonly used with the metric system. On this scale, water freezes at 0 degrees C and boils at 100 degrees C. When you compare the two temperature scales shown, you see that 177 degrees Celsius is the same as 350 degrees Fahrenheit.

The stove in Jackie's kitchen, and probably in yours, too, has a Fahrenheit scale on the oven. However, there is an inexpensive stick-on Celsius scale that can be put on your oven to help you in the future. For the time being, Jackie decides to bake the cookies at 350 degrees Fahrenheit.

6

You in the Metric World

CAN YOU FILL in your own measurements now and join Mark and Jackie in the metric world? You could even try measuring your parents and your friends. Your father might be surprised to hear he weighs 75 kilograms. It does take some time to become familiar with new terms like these, but you are already on your way.

Your height_____centimeters
Your weight_____kilograms
Your waist_____centimeters

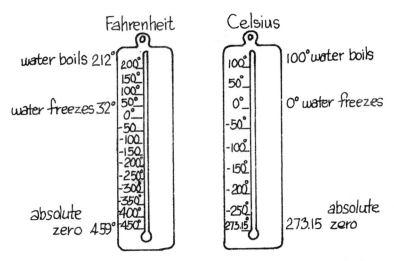

Now you can begin to notice metric terms being used today. Some television weather announcers now give the temperature in Celsius degrees as well as Fahrenheit. For instance, an announcer might say the high in Denver is 80 degrees Fahrenheit, or 27 degrees Celsius.

Some baseball parks now show the distance for home runs in meters as well as in feet. They may have 328 feet or 100 meters painted on the outfield fence. You will know what the sports announcers are talking about when they discuss this, as they often do today.

You also will hear metric terms used by sports announcers during the next Olympic Games. Many of the walking, running, and swimming events are measured in metric units, as well as other events like the 110-meter hurdles and the 70-meter ski jump. When you buy skis, the length usually is given in centimeters.

Watch for signs along the highway that say "New City, 50 kilometers," or "Speed Limit, 100 kilometers per hour." Sounds as if you would be speeding along, doesn't it? But 100 kph would be only 62 miles per hour. If you travel in a foreign country, you will see such signs everywhere.

Speaking of foreign countries, if your parents have a car made in Germany, France, Japan, or some other foreign country, check the owner's manual. The part sizes are given in metric measurements, as is the amount of gas the tank will hold. Mechanics who work on these cars already use metric tools.

Do you have a chemistry set? If so, you can see the weights of various chemicals given in grams or milligrams. Your druggist probably could show you the metric scale he uses to measure out prescriptions. Or you can check a bottle of vitamins. The label usually shows the ingredients in milligrams.

Another place you may find metric measurements used today is in a world atlas. If it gives both miles and kilometers, you can compare and begin to estimate all distances in kilometers. Start thinking about local distances in metric terms. For instance, about how many kilometers is it from your house to school? Or downtown?

When you go to the grocery store, try to think metric. Look at the labels on cans of food and see if you can find the weight in grams. Some packages list grams as well as ounces or pounds. It is easier to use the metric system to tell which of the packages shown below is the better buy.

You could stop and figure out how many ounces there are in 1 lb. 10 oz., but it would take longer than comparing the grams.

There are many ways to try out your skill, and the more practice you get, the better you will be. In a very short time, you can be an expert on the metric system.

All you have learned about the metric system will certainly help you with your math and science classes. Whatever your plans are, your knowledge of the metric system will make a changing world seem less strange. Like Mark and Jackie, you will be better prepared for whatever the future holds for you.

Metric Measurement Summary

PREFIXES
milli = .001
centi = .01
deci = .1
deca = 10
hecto = 100
kilo = 1,000

LENGTH

1,000 milliliters = 1 meter
100 centimeters = 1 meter
10 decimeters = 1 meter
1 decameter = 10 meters
1 hectometer = 100 meters
1 kilometer = 1,000 meters

CAPACITY

1,000 milliliters = 1 liter
100 centiliters = 1 liter
10 deciliters = 1 liter
1 decaliter = 10 liters
1 hectoliter = 100 liters
1 kiloliter = 1,000 liters

WEIGHT

1,000 milligrams = 1 gram
100 centigrams = 1 gram
10 decigrams = 1 gram
1 decagram = 10 grams
1 hectogram = 100 grams
1 kilogram = 1,000 grams
1 metric ton = 1,000 kilograms

Metric-English Equivalents

METRIC TO ENGLISH

1 centimeter = .4 inch
1 meter = 3.3 feet
1 meter = 1.1 yards
1 square meter = 1.2 square yards
1 hectare = 2.5 acres
1 kilometer = .62 mile
1 liter = 2.1 pints
1 liter = 1.1 quarts
1 liter = .26 gallon
1 gram = .04 ounce
1 kilogram = 2.2 pounds
1 metric ton = 2,200 pounds
0 degrees Celsius = 32 degrees Fahrenheit
100 degrees Celsius = 212 degrees Fahrenheit

ENGLISH TO METRIC

1 inch	=	2.5 centimeters
1 foot	=	.3 meter
1 yard	=	.9 meter
1 square yard	=	.8 square meter
1 acre	=	.4 hectare
1 mile	=	1.6 kilometers
1 pint	=	.47 liter
1 quart	=	.95 liter
1 gallon	=	3.8 liters
1 ounce	=	28.3 grams
1 pound	=	.45 kilogram
1 ton	=	.91 metric ton
32 degrees Fahrenheit	=	0 degrees Celsius
212 degrees Fahrenheit	=	100 degrees Celsius

Index